PowerKiDS Readers
MY COMMUNITY
MI COMUNIDAD

A TRIP TO THE LIBRARY

DE VISITA EN LA BIBLIOTECA

Josie Keogh

Traducción al español: Eduardo Alamán

PowerKiDS press™

New York

Published in 2013 by The Rosen Publishing Group, Inc.
29 East 21st Street, New York, NY 10010

First Edition

Editor: Amelie von Zumbusch   Traducción al español: Eduardo Alamán
Book Design: Ashley Drago

Photo Credits: Cover, pp. 5, 6, 9, 21 Shutterstock.com; p. 10 Sam Bloomberg-Rissman/Blend Images/Getty Images; p. 13 Livia Corona/Stone/Getty Images; p. 14 Ableimages/Riser/Getty Images; p. 17 © www.iStockphoto.com/Kyu Oh; p. 18 Andy Crawford/Dorling Kindersley/Getty Images; p. 22 © www.iStockphoto.com/kali9.

Library of Congress Cataloging-in-Publication Data

Keogh, Josie.
 A trip to the library = De visita en la biblioteca / by Josie Keogh. — 1st ed.
   p. cm. — (Powerkids readers: My community = Mi comunidad)
 English and Spanish.
 Translator, Eduardo Alamán.
 Includes index.
 ISBN 978-1-4488-7833-8 (library binding)
 1. Libraries—Juvenile literature. I. Keogh, Josie. Trip to the library. English. II. Keogh, Josie. Trip to the library. Spanish. III. Title. IV. Title: De visita en la biblioteca.

 Z665.5.K4618 2013
 027–dc23

2011049993

Websites: Due to the changing nature of Internet links, PowerKids Press has developed an online list of websites related to the subject of this book. This site is updated regularly. Please use this link to access the list: www.powerkidslinks.com/pkrc/lib/

Manufactured in the United States of America

CPSIA Compliance Information: Batch #CS12PK: For Further Information contact Rosen Publishing, New York, New York at 1-800-237-9932

CONTENTS

CONTENIDO

Mr. Lee's class went to
the library.

La clase del señor Lee fue a
la biblioteca.

5

6

It was fun!

_____

¡Fue muy divertido!

7

Ms. Gray read to them.

La señorita Gray leyó a la clase.

The kids picked books.

_____

Los chicos eligieron algunos libros.

Kim got a book on dogs.

Kim eligió un libro acerca de perros.

Josh found one on cars.

Josh encontró uno
sobre autos.

Matt wanted a book on cats.
Ms. Gray found one.

Matt quería un libro sobre gatos. La señorita Gray encontró uno para Matt.

Ms. Hall checked the books out.

La señorita Hall ayudó a
sacar los libros.

19

The kids took the books home.

Los chicos llevaron sus libros a casa.

21

They will be due in two weeks.

Tienen que regresar los libros en dos semanas.

WORDS TO KNOW / PALABRAS QUE DEBES SABER

fiction: Stories.

ficción: Historias.

librarian: A person who works in a library.

bibliotecaria (o): Persona que trabaja en una biblioteca.

nonfiction: Books of facts.

no ficción: Libros de hechos.